Poems For Christmas

Compiled by Zenka and Ian Woodward

Illustrated by Liz Graham-Yooll

Beaver Books

A Beaver Book
Published by Arrow Books Limited
62-65 Chandos Place, London WC2N 4NW

An imprint of Century Hutchinson Limited

London Melbourne Sydney Auckland
Johannesburg and agencies throughout the world

First published by Hutchinson Children's Books 1984

Beaver edition 1985
Reprinted 1986 and 1989

Set in Linoterm Bembo by
JH Graphics Ltd, Reading

Made and printed in Great Britain by
Courier International Ltd
Tiptree, Essex

ISBN 0 09 973360 9

Hello

Hello, here is a book of verse chosen specially for
   you,
whoever you may be, wherever you are,
some of the poems are old, and some are new,
but each one is glowing like a Christmas star.

Leonard Clark

Christ's nativity

And it came to pass in those days, that there went out a decree from Caesar Augustus, that all the world should be taxed. (And this taxing was first made when Cyrenius was governor of Syria.)

And all went to be taxed, every one into his own city.

And Joseph also went up from Galilee, out of the city of Nazareth, into Judea, unto the city of David, which is called Bethlehem (because he was of the house and lineage of David), to be taxed with Mary his espoused wife, being great with child.

And so it was, that, while they were there, the days were accomplished that she should be delivered. And she brought forth her firstborn son, and wrapped him in swaddling clothes, and laid him in a manger; because there was no room for them in the inn.

The Bible
(Luke 2: 1–7)

Something beautiful and new and strange
(from *The Witnesses*)

The Innkeeper's wife:
   It was a night in winter.
Our house was full, tight-packed as salted herrings –
So full, they said, we had to hold our breaths
To close the door and shut the night-air out!
And then two travellers came. They stood outside
Across the threshold, half in the ring of light
And half beyond it. I would have let them in
Despite the crowding – the woman was past her
   time –
But I'd no mind to argue with my husband,
The flagon in my hand and half the inn
Still clamouring for wine. But when trade
   slackened,
And all our guests had sung themselves to bed
Or told the floor their troubles, I came out here
Where he had lodged them. The man was standing
As you are now, his hand smoothing that board.
He was a carpenter, I heard them say.
She rested on the straw, and on her arm
A child was lying. None of your creased-faced brats
Squalling their lungs out. Just lying there
As calm as a new-dropped calf – his eyes wide open,
And gazing round as if the world he saw
In the chaff-strewn light of the stable lantern
Was something beautiful and new and strange.

Clive Sansom

5

Little child in a manger

I saw a stable, low and very bare,
    A little child in a manger.
The oxen knew him, had him in their care,
    To men he was a stranger.
The safety of the world was lying there,
    And the world's danger.

Mary Coleridge

It was on Christmas Day

It was on Christmas Day,
And all in the morning,
Our Saviour was born,
And our heavenly King:
And was not this a joyful thing?
And sweet Jesus they called him by name.

Salute the happy morn

Christians, awake, salute the happy morn,
On which the Saviour of mankind was born.

Softly the night

Softly the night is sleeping on Bethlehem's peaceful
  hill,
Silent the shepherds watching their gentle flocks are
  still.
But hark the wondrous music falls from the
  opening sky,
Valley and cliff re-echo glory to God on high.
Glory to God it rings again,
Peace on the earth, goodwill to men.

Come with the gladsome shepherds quick
  hastening from the fold,
Come with the wise men bringing incense and
  myrrh and gold,
Come to him poor and lowly all round the cradle
  throng,
Come with our hearts of sunshine and sing the
  angels' song.
Glory to God tell out again,
Peace on the earth, goodwill to men.

Wave you the wreath unfading, the fir tree and the
  pine,
Green from the snows of winter to deck the holy
  shrine;
Bring you the happy children for this is Christmas
  morn,
Jesus the sinless infant, Jesus the Lord is born.
Glory to God, to God again,
Peace on the earth, goodwill to men.

The donkey's Christmas

Plodding on,
From inn to inn,
No room to spare,
No room but a stable bare.
We rest,
And the following morning Jesus is born.
I gaze on the wondrous sight.
The King is born,
The King in a stable.
I see great lights,
Lights that are angels.
Everyone comes to see this sight.
I carried Mary,
Holy Mary,
Last night.

The friendly beasts

Jesus our brother, kind and good,
Was humbly born in a stable rude,
And the friendly beasts around him stood;
Jesus our brother, kind and good.

'I,' said the donkey, shaggy and brown,
'I carried his mother up hill and down,
I carried her safely to Bethlehem town;
I,' said the donkey, shaggy and brown.

'I,' said the cow, all white and red,
'I gave him my manger for his bed,
I gave him my hay to pillow his head;
I,' said the cow, all white and red.

'I,' said the sheep, with the curly horn,
'I gave him my wool for his blanket warm;
He wore my coat on Christmas morn.
I,' said the sheep with the curly horn.

'I,' said the dove, from the rafters high,
'Cooed him to sleep, my mate and I,
We cooed him to sleep, my mate and I;
I,' said the dove, from the rafters high.

And every beast, by some good spell,
In the stable dark, was glad to tell,
Of the gift he gave Emmanuel,
The gift he gave Emmanuel.

Before the paling of the stars

Before the paling of the stars,
  Before the winter morn,
Before the earliest cock crow,
  Jesus Christ was born:
Born in a stable,
  Cradled in a manger,
In the world his hands had made
  Born a stranger.

Priest and king lay fast asleep
  In Jerusalem;
Young and old lay fast asleep
  In crowded Bethlehem;
Saint and angel, ox and ass,
  Kept a watch together
Before the Christmas daybreak
  In the winter weather.

Jesus on his mother's breast
  In the stable cold,
Spotless lamb of God was he,
  Shepherd of the fold:
Let us kneel with Mary maid,
  With Joseph bent and hoary,
With saint and angel, ox and ass,
  To hail the King of Glory.

Christina Rossetti

St Joseph and God's Mother

St Joseph and God's Mother,
   They kept good company,
And they rode out of Nazareth
   So early in the day.

They found no place to rest in,
   No place in all the town,
And so they made an arbour,
   Of reeds and grasses brown.

St Joseph went to look for fire,
   No fire there could he see,
And when he came to Mary,
   The babe was on her knee,
As white as is the milk,
   As red as rose was he.

St Joseph looked upon him:
   'O what is this fair thing?
This is no child of mine,
   This comes from heaven's King.'

By there came three shepherds
   To wish him a good day,
The two upon their fiddles,
   The third his bells did play.

And there they played sweet music,
   All for to make him mirth;
Three hours have not gone yet
   Since our Saviour's birth.

'Dance, Maiden Mary,
    Dance, Mother mild,
And if you will dance with me,
    The ass will hold the Child.'

'I will not dance, Joseph,
    My Husband so dear,
But if you will dance for joy,
    Dance, husband, here.'

Joseph then began to dance
    With all his might and main;
The mother smiled and said to him
    'Joseph is young again.'

'And if I rejoice, Mary,
    Well ought that to be;
Here is born to us tonight
    The King of glory.'

Welcome to Heaven's King

Welcome be thou, Heaven's King,
Welcome, born in one morning;
Welcome, for him we shall sing –
    Welcome, Yule!

O little town

O little town of Bethlehem
   How still we see thee lie!
Above the deep and dreamless sleep
   The silent stars go by.
Yet in thy dark streets shineth
   The everlasting light;
The hopes and fears of all the years
   Are met in thee tonight.

O morning stars, together
   Proclaim the holy birth,
And praises sing to God the King,
   And peace to men on earth;
For Christ is born of Mary;
   And, gathered all above,
While mortals sleep, the angels keep
   Their watch of wondering love.

How silently, how silently,
   The wondrous gift is given!
So God imparts to human hearts
   The blessings of his heaven.
No ear may hear his coming;
   But in this world of sin,
Where meek souls will receive him, still
   The dear Christ enters in.

Where children pure and happy
  Pray to the blessed Child,
Where misery cries out to thee,
  Son of the mother mild:
Where charity stands watching
  And faith holds wide the door,
The dark night wakes, the glory breaks,
  And Christmas comes once more.

O holy Child of Bethlehem,
  Descend to us, we pray;
Cast out our sin, and enter in,
  Be born in us today.
We hear the Christmas angels
  The great glad tidings tell:
O come to us, abide with us,
  Our Lord Emmanuel.

Bishop Phillips Brooks

Redeemer of mankind

O Come, Redeemer of mankind, appear,
Thee with full hearts the Virgin-born we greet:
Let every age with rapt amazement hear
That wondrous birth which for our God is meet.

Ambrose, Bishop of Milan

Rejoice and be merry

Rejoice and be merry in songs and in mirth!
O praise our Redeemer, all mortals on earth!
For this is the birthday of Jesus our King,
Who brought us salvation – his praises we'll sing!

A heavenly vision appeared in the sky;
Vast numbers of angels the shepherds did spy,
Proclaiming the birthday of Jesus our King,
Who brought us salvation – his praises we'll sing!

Likewise a bright star in the sky did appear,
Which led the Wise Men from the east to draw near;
They found the Messiah, sweet Jesus our King,
Who brought us salvation – his praises we'll sing!

And when they were come, they their treasures
    unfold,
And unto him offered myrrh, incense, and gold.
So blessed for ever be Jesus our King,
Who brought us salvation – his praises we'll sing.

Nativity

Angels, from the realms of glory,
  Wing your flight o'er all the earth,
You who sang creation's story,
  Now proclaim Messiah's birth;
    Come and worship,
Worship Christ the new-born King.

Shepherds, in the field abiding,
  Watching over your flocks by night,
God with man is now residing,
  Yonder shines the infant-light;
    Come and worship,
Worship Christ the new-born King.

Sages, leave your contemplations,
  Brighter visions beam afar;
Seek the great desire of nations;
  You have seen his natal star;
    Come and worship,
Worship Christ the new-born King.

Saints before the altar bending,
  Watching long in hope and fear,
Suddenly the Lord, descending,
  In his temple shall appear;
    Come and worship,
Worship Christ the new-born King.

Sinners, wrung with true repentance,
  Doomed for guilt to endless pains,
Justice now revokes the sentence,
  Mercy calls you – break your chains;
    Come and worship,
Worship Christ the new-born King.

James Montgomery

Joseph and Jesus

Said Joseph unto Mary,
    'Be counselled by me:
Fetch your love child from the manger,
    For to Egypt we must flee.'

As Mary went a–riding
    Up the hill out of view,
The ass was much astonished
    How like a dove he flew.

Said Jesus unto Joseph,
    Who his soft cheek did kiss:
'There are thorns in your beard, good sir.
    I asked not for this.'

Then Joseph brought to Jesus
    Hot paps of white bread
Which, when it burned that pretty mouth,
    Joseph swallowed in his stead.

Robert Graves
(from the Spanish)

The miraculous harvest

'Rise up, rise up, you merry men all,
   See that you ready be:
All children under two years old
   Now slain they all shall be.'

Then Jesus, yes, and Joseph,
   And Mary that was unknown,
They travelled by a husbandman,
   Just while his seed was sown.

'God speed your work,' said Jesus,
   'Throw all your seed away,
And carry home as ripened corn
   What you have sown this day;

'For to keep your wife and family
   From sorrow, grief and pain,
And keep Christ in remembrance
   Till seed-time comes again.'

The husbandman fell on his knees,
   Even upon his face;
'Long time have you been looked for,
   But now you've come at last.

'And I myself do now believe
   Your name is Jesus called;
Redeemer of mankind are you,
   Though undeserving all.'

After that there came King Herod,
    With his train so furiously,
Enquiring of the husbandman
    Whether Jesus had passed by.

'Why, the truth it must be spoke,
    And the truth it must be known,
For Jesus he passed by this way,
    Just as my seed was sown.

'But now I have it reapen,
    And some laid in my wain,
Ready to fetch and carry
    Into my barn again.'

'Turn back,' then says the Captain,
    'Your labour and mine's in vain;
It's full three quarters of a year
    Since he his seed has sown.'

So Herod was deceived
    By the work of God's own hand:
No further he proceeded
    Into the Holy Land.

There's thousands of children young,
    Which for his sake did die;
Do not forbid those little ones,
    And do not them deny.

As Mary was a-walking

As Mary was a-walking
    By Bethlehem one day,
Her Son was in her arms,
    So heavenly to see.

'O give me water, Mother.'
    'You cannot drink, my dear;
For the rivers they are muddy,
    And the streams they are not clear;

'The rivers they are muddy,
    And the streams they are not clear,
And the springs are full of blood,
    You cannot drink from here.'

They came into a grove,
    So thick with oranges
That not another orange
    Could hang upon the trees;
There sat a man to guard them,
    Was blind in both his eyes.

'Give me an orange, blind man,
    To feed my Son today.'
'And take as many, lady,
    As you can bear away;

'Gather the biggest, lady,
    That most are to your mind,
The small ones soon will ripen,
    If you leave them behind.'

They gathered them by one and one,
    There grew a hundred more,
And straight the man began to see
    That had been blind before.

'O who is this fair lady,
    Has made me see again?'
It was the Holy Virgin
    That walked by Bethlehem.

The birds

When Jesus Christ was four years old,
The angels brought him toys of gold,
Which no man ever had bought or sold.

And yet with these he would not play.
He made him small fowl out of clay,
And blessed them till they flew away:
Tu creasti Domine.

Jesus Christ, thou child so wise,
Bless mine hands and fill mine eyes,
And bring my soul to Paradise.

Hilaire Belloc

Robin's song

Robins sang in England,
    Frost or rain or snow,
All the long December days
    Endless years ago.

Robins sang in England
    Before the Legions came,
Before our English fields were tilled
    Or England was a name.

Robins sang in England
    When forests dark and wild
Stretched across from sea to sea
    And Jesus was a child.

Listen! in the frosty dawn
    From his leafless bough
The same brave song he ever sang
    A robin's singing now.

Rodney Bennett

Robin Redbreast

Welcome Robin with your greeting,
On the threshold meekly waiting,
To the children's home now enter,
From the cold and snow of winter,
From the cold and snow of winter.

Are you cold? or are you hungry?
Pretty Robin, don't be angry,
All the children round you rally,
While the snow is in the valley,
While the snow is in the valley.

Come in, Robin, do not fear us,
Your bright eye and chirping cheer us;
Your sad notes excite our pity,
Now the frost begins to bite you,
Now the frost begins to bite you.

Robin come and tell your story,
Leave outside your care and worry;
Tell the children, Robin dearest,
Of the babies in the forest,
Of the babies in the forest.

Of the flame that burnt your bosom,
Of your wanderings far and lonesome,
Of your home among the greenwood,
Of your happy days of childhood,
Of your happy days of childhood.

Bread and milk

Bread and milk for breakfast,
   And woollen frocks to wear,
And a crumb for Robin Redbreast
   On the cold days of the year.

Christina Rossetti

Snow clouds

Like sulky polar bears
Clouds prowl across the winter sky
From cold and snowy northern lands
As though from icy lairs.

Soon snow begins to fall –
Small snippets of the whitest fur
And like the stealthy polar bear
It makes no sound at all.

Daphne Lister

Snowing

Snowing; snowing;
Oh, between earth and sky
A wintry wind is blowing,
Scattering with its sigh
Petals from trees of silver that shine
Like invisible glass, when the moon
In the void of night on high
Paces her orchards divine.

Snowing; snowing;
Ah me, how still, and how fair
The air with flakes interflowing,
The fields crystal and bare,
When the brawling brooks are dumb
And the parched trees matted with frost,
And the birds in this wilderness stare
Dazzled and num'd!

Snowing . . . snowing . . . snowing:
Moments of time through space
Into hours, centuries growing,
Till the world's marred lovely face,
Wearied of change and chance,
Radiant in innocent dream –
Lulled by an infinite grace
To rest in eternal trance.

Walter de la Mare

A singing in the air
(from *Christmas at Freelands*)

A snowy field! A stable piled
With straw! A donkey's sleepy pow!★
A Mother beaming on a Child!
A Manger, and a munching cow!
– These we all remember now –
And airy voices, heard afar!
And three Magicians, and a Star!

Two thousand times of snow declare
That on the Christmas of the year
There is a singing in the air;
And all who listen for it hear
A fairy chime, a seraph strain,
Telling He is born again,
– That all we love is born again.

James Stephens

★[An old Scottish word meaning 'head']

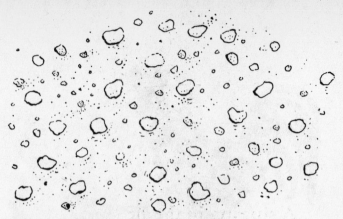

The land of snow

Snow . . . snow . . . eternally falling:
Armies in white, crossing the grey-blue air
In endless downward procession, falling and falling.

Snow on the swift deer, the running deer of the
    forest;
On sledges that travel the hidden roads faster than
    wolves that follow;
Snow on a frozen lake and the Snow Queen's palace
    of ice.

All is a world of whiteness: Earth with her winter
    blossom,
Sky her incessant snowflakes . . . Ah, but look
Forging south, opposing the white relentless
    legions,
There flies a single crow, calling and calling.

Clive Sansom

Cock-crow at Christmas
(from *Hamlet*)

Some say that ever 'gainst that season comes
Wherein our Saviour's birth is celebrated,
The bird of dawning singeth all night long;
And then, they say, no spirit can walk abroad;
The nights are wholesome; then no planets strike,
No fairy takes, nor witch hath power to charm,
So hallowed and so gracious is the time.

William Shakespeare

In the bleak mid-winter

In the bleak mid-winter
   Frosty wind made moan,
Earth stood hard as iron,
   Water like a stone;
Snow had fallen, snow on snow,
   Snow on snow,
In the bleak mid-winter
   Long ago.

Our God, Heaven cannot hold him
   Nor earth sustain;
Heaven and earth shall flee away
   When he comes to reign;
In the bleak mid-winter
   A stable-place sufficed
The Lord God Almighty
   Jesus Christ.

Enough for him, whom cherubim
   Worship night and day,
A breastful of milk
   And a mangerful of hay;
Enough for him, whom angels
   Fall down before,
The ox and ass and camel
   Which adore.

Angels and archangels
   May have gathered there,
Cherubim and seraphim
   Thronged the air;
But only his mother
   In her maiden bliss
Worshipped the Beloved
   With a kiss.

What can I give him,
   Poor as I am?
If I were a shepherd
   I would bring a lamb,
If I were a Wise Man
   I would do my part –
Yet what I can, I give him,
   Give my heart.

Christina Rossetti

The burning babe

As I in hoary winter's night
  Stood shivering in the snow,
Surprised I was with sudden heat
  Which made my heart to glow;
And lifting up a fearful eye
  To view what fire was near,
A pretty babe all burning bright
  Did in the air appear;
Who, scorchéd with excessive heat,
  · Such floods of tears did shed,
As though his floods should quench his flames,
  Which with his tears were fed.
'Alas!' quoth he, 'but newly born
  In fiery heats I fry,
Yet none approach to warm their hearts
  Or feel my fire but I!

'My faultless breast the furnace is;
    The fuel, wounding thorns;
Love is the fire, and sighs the smoke;
    The ashes, shames and scorns;
The fuel Justice layeth on,
    And Mercy blows the coals,
The metal in this furnace wrought
    Are men's defiléd souls:
For which, as now on fire I am
    To work them to their good,
So will I melt into their bath,
    To wash them in my blood.'
With this he vanished out of sight
    And swiftly shrunk away,
And straight I called unto mind
    That it was Christmas Day.

Robert Southwell

Jingle bells

Dashing through the snow,
In a one–horse open sleigh;
O'er the fields we go,
Laughing all the way;
Bells on bob–tail ring.
Making spirits bright;
Oh what fun to ride and sing
A sleighing song tonight.

REFRAIN:

Jingle bells, jingle bells,
Jingle all the way;
Oh! What joy it is to ride
In a one-horse open sleigh.
Jingle bells, jingle bells,
Jingle all the way.
Oh! What joy it is to ride
In a one-horse open sleigh.

A day or two ago
I thought I'd take a ride,
And soon Miss Fannie Bright
Was seated by my side.
The horse was lean and lank;
Misfortune seemed his lot;
He got into a drifted bank,
And we, we got up-sot.

[*REFRAIN*]

A day or two ago
The story I must tell
I went out in the snow
And on my back I fell;
A gent was riding by
In a one-horse open sleigh
He laughed as there I sprawling lie,
And quickly drove away.

[*REFRAIN*]

Now the ground is white;
Go it while you're young;
Take the girls tonight,
And sing this sleighing song.
Just get a bob-tailed bay,
Two forty as his speed;
Hitch him to an open sleigh,
And crack, you'll take the lead.

[*REFRAIN*]

James Pierpont

Winter morning

Winter is the king of showmen,
Turning tree stumps into snowmen
And houses into birthday cakes
And spreading sugar over lakes.
Smooth and clean and frosty white,
The world looks good enough to bite.
That's the season to be young,
Catching snowflakes on your tongue.

Snow is snowy when it's snowing,
I'm sorry it's slushy when it's going.

Ogden Nash

When all the world is full of snow

I never know
just where to go,
when all the world
is full of snow.

I do not want
to make a track,
not even
to the shed and back.

I only want
to watch and wait,
while snow moths settle
on the gate,

and swarming frost flakes
fill the trees
with billions
of albino bees.

I want to watch
the snow swarms thin,
'til all my bees
have settled in,

and on the ice
the boulders ride,
like sleeping snow geese
on the tide.

I only want
myself to be
as silent as
a winter tree,

to hear the swirling
stillness grow,
when all the world
is full of snow.

       N. M. Bodecker

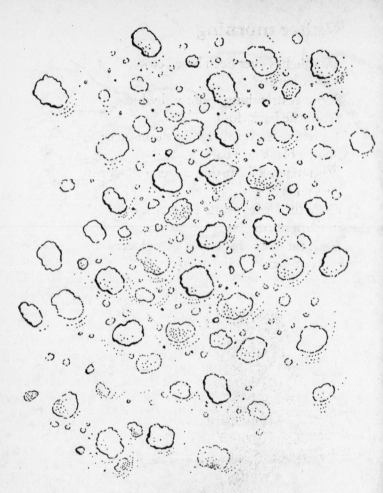

I could eat it!

I could eat it!
This snow that falls
      So softly, so softly.

Kobayashi Issa

Winter morning

No one has ever been here before,
Never before!
Snow is stretching, pure and white,
From the back door
To where that elm-tree by the coppice-fence
Stands black and bare,
With never a footprint, never a clawprint
Anywhere!
Only the clean, white page of snow
In front of me,
With the long shadow of a single tree
For company.

Clive Sansom

Blue toboggans

scarves for the apaches
wet gloves for snowballs
whoops for white clouds
and blue toboggans

stamping for a tingle
lamps for four o'clock
steamed glass for buses
and blue toboggans

tuning-forks for Wenceslas
white fogs for Prestwick
mince pies for the Eventides
and blue toboggans

TV for the lonely
a long haul for heaven
a shilling for the gas
and blue toboggans

Edwin Morgan

Chill December

Chill December brings the sleet,
Blazing fire, and Christmas treat.

Sara Coleridge

Christmas Star

It was winter.
The wind blew from the steppe
And it was cold for the child
In the cave on the hillside.

He was warmed by the breath of an ox.
The farm animals
Were stabled in the cave,
And a warm haze drifted over the manger.

Shaking from their sheepskins
The wisps of straw and hay-seeds of their bedding,
Half asleep, the shepherds gazed
From a rock ledge into the midnight distance.

Far away were a snowy field, a graveyard,
Fences, tombstones,
The shaft of a cart in a snowdrift,
And above the graveyard the sky full of stars.

Near, never seen till then, more shy
Than the glimmer in the window
Of a watchman's hut,
The star shone on its way to Bethlehem.

It flamed like a hayrick,
Standing aside from the sky
And from God;
Glowed like a farm on fire,

Rose like a blazing
Stack of straw.
The sight of the new star
Startled the universe.

Its reddening glow
Was a sign; the three star-gazers
Hurried to the call
Of its unprecedented light.

Camels followed them loaded with gifts,
And donkeys in harness, one smaller than the other,
Minced down the hill.

In a strange vision all time to come
Arose in the distance:
All the thoughts, hopes, worlds of the centuries,
The future of art galleries and of museums,
All the pranks of goblins and deeds of magicians,
All the Christmas trees and all the children's dreams:

The shimmering candles, the paper chains,
The splendour of coloured tinsel . . .
. . . Angrier and more wicked blew the wind from
    the steppe . . .
. . . All the apples and golden bubbles.

Part of the pond was hidden by the alders,
But from where the shepherds stood
A part could be seen between the rooks' nests in the
    treetops.

They watched camels and donkeys skirting the
    pool.
'Let's go with the others,' they said,
Wrapping themselves in their sheepskins,
'Let's bow to the miracle.'

They grew hot from shuffling in the snow.
On the bright plain bare footsteps,
Shining like glass, led round the hut.
In the starlight the sheepdogs growled at these
    tracks,
As though they were burning candle-ends.

The frosty night was like a fairy-tale.
Invisible beings kept stepping down
From the snowdrifts into the crowd.

The dogs followed, looking round apprehensively;
They kept close to the youngest shepherd,
    expecting trouble.

Through the same countryside, along the same
    road,
Several angels walked among the crowd.
Bodiless beings, they were invisible;
Only their steps left a trace.

A crowd had gathered by the stone at the entrance.
Day was breaking. The trunks of the cedars were
    plain.
'Who are you?' asked Mary.

'We are a company of shepherds and envoys from
    heaven.
We have come to praise you both.'
'You can't all come in at once. Wait a little by the
    door.'

Shepherds and herdsmen stamped about
In the ashy dusk before the dawn.
By the wooden water-trough
Men on foot and horsemen swore at each other,
Camels roared and asses kicked.

Day was breaking. The dawn swept the remaining
    stars
Like cinders from the sky.
Out of all the great gathering Mary allowed
Only the Wise Men through the opening in the
    rock.

He slept in the oak manger,
Radiant as moonlight in the hollow of a tree.
Instead of a sheepskin,
The lips of the ass and the nostrils of the ox kept him
    warm.

The Magi stood in the shadow,
Whispering, scarcely finding words.
All at once, a hand stretched out of the dark,
Moved one of them aside to the left of the manger:
He looked round. Gazing at the Virgin from the
  doorway
Like a guest, was the Christmas Star.

Boris Pasternak

Make we merry

Make we merry, both more and less,
For now is the time of Christmas.

Let no man come into this hall,
Nor groom, nor page, not yet marshal,
But that some sport he bring withal.

If that he say he cannot sing,
Some other sport then let him bring,
That it may please at this feasting.

If he say he naught can do,
Then, for my love, ask him no mo'
But to the stocks then let him go.

Make we merry, both more and less,
For now is the time of Christmas.

Christmas is coming

Christmas is coming,
  The geese are getting fat,
Please to put a penny
  In the old man's hat.
If you haven't got a penny,
  A ha'penny will do;
If you haven't got a ha'penny,
  Then God bless you!

Christmas comes but once a year

Christmas comes but once a year,
And when it comes it brings good cheer —
A pocket full of money, and a cellar full of beer.

Merry Christmas

Christmas comes! He comes, he comes,
Ushered with a rain of plums;
Hollies in the window greet him;
Schools come driving past to meet him,
Gifts precede him, bells proclaim him,
Every mouth delights to name him;
Wet, and cold, and wind, and dark,
Make him but the warmer mark;
And yet he comes not one–embodied,
Universal's the blithe godhead,
And in every festal house
Presence hath ubiquitous.
Curtains, those snug room–enfolders,
Hang upon his million shoulders,
And he has a million eyes
Of fire, and eats a million pies,
And is very merry and wise;
Very wise and very merry,
And loves a kiss beneath the berry.

Leigh Hunt

Somewhere around Christmas

Always, or nearly always, on old apple trees,
Somewhere around Christmas, if you look up
    through the frost,
You will see, fat as a bullfinch, stuck on a high
    branch,
One, lingering, bald, self sufficient, hard, blunt
    fruit.

There will be no leaves, you can be sure of that;
The twigs will be tar-black, and the white sky
Will be grabbed among the branches like thumbed
    glass
In broken triangles just saved from crashing to the
    ground.

Further up, dribbles of rain will run down
Like spilt colourless varnish on a canvas. The old
    tins,
Tyres, cardboard boxes, debris of back gardens,
Will lie around, bleak, with mould and rust creeping
    over them.

Blow on your fingers. Wipe your feet on the mat by
  the back door.
You will never see that apple fall. Look at the cat,
Her whiskers twitch as she sleeps by the kitchen fire;
In her backyard prowling dream she thinks it's a
  bird.

John Smith

The twelve days of Christmas

The first day of Christmas
My true love sent to me
A partridge in a pear-tree.

The second day of Christmas
My true love sent to me
Two turtle-doves
And a partridge in a pear-tree.

The third day of Christmas
My true love sent to me
Three French hens,
Two turtle-doves
And a partridge in a pear-tree.

The fourth day of Christmas
My true love sent to me
Four colly birds,
Three French hens,
Two turtle-doves
And a partridge in a pear-tree.

The fifth day of Christmas
My true love sent to me
Five gold rings,
Four colly birds,
Three French hens,
Two turtle-doves
And a partridge in a pear-tree.

The sixth day of Christmas
My true love sent to me
Six geese a-laying,
Five gold rings,
Four colly birds,
Three French hens,
Two turtle-doves
And a partridge in a pear-tree.

The seventh day of Christmas
My true love sent to me
Seven swans a-swimming,
Six geese a-laying,
Five gold rings,
Four colly birds,
Three French hens,
Two turtle-doves
And a partridge in a pear-tree.

The eighth day of Christmas
My true love sent to me
Eight maids a-milking,
Seven swans a-swimming,
Six geese a-laying,
Five gold rings,
Four colly birds,
Three French hens,
Two turtle-doves
And a partridge in a pear-tree.

The ninth day of Christmas
My true love sent to me
Nine drummers drumming,
Eight maids a-milking,
Seven swans a-swimming,
Six geese a-laying,
Five gold rings,
Four colly birds,
Three French hens,
Two turtle doves
And a partridge in a pear-tree.

The tenth day of Christmas
My true love sent to me
Ten pipers piping,
Nine drummers drumming,
Eight maids a-milking,
Seven swans a-swimming,
Six geese a-laying,
Five gold rings,
Four colly birds,
Three French hens,
Two turtle-doves
And a partridge in a pear-tree.

The eleventh day of Christmas
My true love sent to me
Eleven ladies dancing,
Ten pipers piping,
Nine drummers drumming,
Eight maids a-milking,
Seven swans a-swimming,
Six geese a-laying,
Five gold rings,
Four colly birds,
Three French hens,
Two turtle-doves
And a partridge in a pear-tree.

The twelfth day of Christmas
My true love sent to me
Twelve lords a-leaping,
Eleven ladies dancing,
Ten pipers piping,
Nine drummers drumming,
Eight maids a-milking,
Seven swans a-swimming,
Six geese a-laying,
Five gold rings,
Four colly birds,
Three French hens,
Two turtle-doves
And a partridge in a pear-tree.

Ceremonies for Christmas

Come, bring with a noise,
My merry, merry boys,
The Christmas log to the firing;
While my good dame, she
Bids you all be free;
And drink to your heart's desiring.

With the last year's brand
Light the new block, and
For good success in his spending,
On your psalteries play,
That sweet luck may
Come while the log is a-tending.

Drink now the strong beer,
Cut the white loaf here,
The while the meat is shredding;
For the rare mince-pie
And the plums stand by
To fill the paste that's a-kneading.

Robert Herrick

Christmas almost come

St Thomas's Day is past and gone,
And Christmas almost come,
    Maidens arise,
      And make your pies,
And save young Bobby some.

Mincemeat

Sing a song of mincemeat,
Currants, raisins, spice,
Apples, sugar, nutmeg,
Everything that's nice,
Stir it with a ladle,
Wish a lovely wish,
Drop it in the middle
Of your well-filled dish,
Stir again for good luck,
Pack it all away
Tied in little jars and pots,
Until Christmas Day.

Elizabeth Gould

Welcome Yule

Now, thrice welcome Christmas,
    Which brings us good cheer,
Mince pies and plum porridge,
    Good ale and strong beer;
With pig, goose, and capon,
    The best that can be,
So well does the weather
    And our stomachs agree.

Observe how the chimneys
    Do smoke all about,
The cooks are providing
    For dinner no doubt;
But those on whose tables
    No victuals appear,
O may they keep Lent
    All the rest of the year!

With holly and ivy
    So green and so gay,
We deck up our houses
    As fresh as the day.
With bays and rosemary,
    And laurel complete;
And everyone now
    Is a king in conceit.

George Wither

A bunch of holly

But give me holly, bold and jolly,
Honest, prickly, shining holly;
Pluck me holly leaf and berry
For the day when I make merry.

Christina Rossetti

Holly

Its head it points to heaven
And shows its berries red
In token of the drops of blood
Which on Calvary were shed.

And in the holly prickles
You can plainly see
The crown of thorns our Saviour wore
When going up to Calvary.

And although up in heaven
His love can still be seen
In the holly colour,
The everlasting green.

The holly and the ivy

The holly and the ivy,
When they are both full grown,
Of all the trees that are in the wood,
The holly bears the crown:

> *REFRAIN:*
> *The rising of the sun*
> *And the running of the deer,*
> *The playing of the merry organ,*
> *Sweet singing in the choir.*

The holly bears a blossom,
As white as lily flower,
And Mary bore sweet Jesus Christ,
To be our sweet Saviour:

> [*REFRAIN*]

The holly bears a berry,
As red as any blood,
And Mary bore sweet Jesus Christ
To do poor sinners good:

> [*REFRAIN*]

The holly bears a prickle,
As sharp as any thorn,
And Mary bore sweet Jesus Christ
On Christmas day in the morn:

[*REFRAIN*]

The holly bears a bark,
As bitter as any gall,
And Mary bore sweet Jesus Christ
For to redeem us all:

[*REFRAIN*]

The holly and the ivy,
When they are both full grown,
Of all the trees that are in the wood
The holly bears the crown.

Gathering in the Christmas mistletoe

The damsel donned her kirtle sheen;
The hall was dressed with holly green;
Forth to the wood did merry-men go,
To gather in the mistletoe.

Sir Walter Scott

Mistletoe

Sitting under the mistletoe
(Pale green, fairy mistletoe),
One last candle burning low,
All the sleepy dancers gone,
Just one candle burning on,
Shadows lurking everywhere:
Someone came, and kissed me there.

Tired I was; my head would go
Nodding under the mistletoe
(Pale green, fairy mistletoe),
No footsteps came, no voice, but only,
Just as I sat there, sleepy, lonely,
Stooped in the still and shadowy air
Lips unseen – and kissed me there.

Walter de la Mare

Planting mistletoe

Let the old tree be the gold tree;
Hand up the silver seed:
Let the hoary tree be the glory tree,
To shine out at need,
At mirth-time, at dearth-time,
Gold bough and milky bead.

For the root's failing and the shoot's failing;
Soon it will bloom no more.
The growth's arrested, the yaffle's* nested
Deep in its hollow core:
Over the grasses thinly passes
The shade so dark before.

Save a few sprigs of the new twigs,
If any such you find:
Don't lose them, but use them,
Keeping a good kind
To be rooting and fruiting
When this is old and blind.

So the tragic tree is the magic tree,
Running the whole range
Of growing and blowing
And suffering change:
Then buying, by dying,
The wonderful and strange.

Ruth Pitter

*[The green woodpecker]

The Christmas Tree

Put out the lights now!
Look at the Tree, the rough tree dazzled
In oriole plumes of flame,
Tinselled with twinkling frost fire, tasselled
With stars and moons – the same
That yesterday hid in the spinney and had no fame
Till we put out the lights now.

Hard are the nights now:
The fields at moonrise turn to agate,
Shadows are cold as jet;
In dyke and furrow, in copse and faggot
The frost's tooth is set;
And stars are the sparks whirled out by the north
    wind's fret
On the flinty nights now.

So feast your eyes now
On mimic star and moon–cold bauble:
Worlds may wither unseen,
But the Christmas Tree is a tree of fable,
A phoenix in evergreen,
And the world cannot change or chill what its
    mysteries mean
To your hearts and eyes now.

The vision dies now
Candle by candle: the tree that embraced it
Returns to its own kind,
To be earthed again and weather as best it
May the frost and the wind.
Children, it too had its hour – you will not mind
If it lives or dies now.

C. Day Lewis

Little silent Christmas tree

little tree
little silent Christmas tree
you are so little
you are more like a flower

who found you in the green forest
and were you very sorry to come away?
see   i will comfort you
because you smell so sweetly

i will kiss your cool bark
and hug you safe and tight
just as your mother would,
only don't be afraid

look   the spangles
that sleep all the year in a dark box
dreaming of being taken out and allowed to shine,
the balls the chains red and gold the fluffy threads,

put up your little arms
and i'll give them all to you to hold
every finger shall have its ring
and there won't be a single place dark or unhappy

then when you're quite dressed
you'll stand in the window for everyone to see
and how they'll stare!
oh but you'll be very proud

and my little sister and i will take hands
and looking up at our beautiful tree
we'll dance and sing
'Noël Noël'

e. e. cummings

Advice to a child

Set your fir-tree
In a pot;
Needles green
Is all it's got.
Shut the door
And go away,
And so to sleep
Till Christmas Day.
In the morning
Seek your tree,
And you shall see
What you shall see.

Hang your stocking
By the fire,
Empty of
Your heart's desire;
Up the chimney
Say your say,
And so to sleep
Till Christmas Day.
In the morning
Draw the blind,
And you shall find
What you shall find.

Eleanor Farjeon

Christmas in a village

Each house is swept the day before,
And windows stuck with evergreens;
The snow is besomed from the door,
And comfort crowns the cottage scenes.
Gilt holly with its thorny pricks
And yew and box with berries small,
These deck the unused candlesticks,
And pictures hanging by the wall.

Neighbours resume their annual cheer,
Wishing with smiles and spirits high
Glad Christmas and a happy year
To every morning passer-by.
Milkmaids their Christmas journeys go
Accompanied with favoured swain,
And children pace the crumping snow
To taste their granny's cake again.

Hung with the ivy's veining bough,
The ash trees round the cottage farm
Are often stripped of branches now
The cottar's Christmas hearth to warm.
He swings and twists his hazel band,
And lops them off with sharpened hook,
And oft brings ivy in his hand
To decorate the chimney nook . . .

The shepherd now no more afraid,
Since custom does the chance bestow,
Starts up to kiss the giggling maid
Beneath the branch of mistletoe
That 'neath each cottage beam is seen
With pearl-like berries shining gay,
The shadow still of what has been
Which fashion yearly fades away.

And singers too, a merry throng,
At early morn with simple skill
Yet imitate the angel's song
And chant their Christmas ditty still;
And 'mid the storm that dies and swells
By fits – in hummings softly steals
The music of the village bells
Ringing round their merry peals.

And when it's past, a merry crew
Bedecked in masks and ribbons gay,
The morris dance their sports renew
And act their winter evening play.
The clown-turned-king for penny praise
Storms with the actor's strut and swell,
And Harlequin a laugh to raise
Wears his hunchback and tinkling bell.

And oft for pence and spicy ale
With winter nosegays pinned before,
The wassail singer tells her tale
And drawls her Christmas carols o'er,
While prentice boy with ruddy face
And frost–bepowdered dancing locks
From door to door with happy pace
Runs round to claim his Christmas box.

John Clare

Singing in the streets

I had almost forgotten the singing in the streets,
Snow piled up by the houses, drifting
Underneath the door into the warm room,
Firelight, lamplight, the little lame cat
Dreaming in soft sleep on the hearth, mother
    dozing,
Waiting for Christmas to come, the boys and me
Trudging over blanket fields waving lanterns to the
    sky.
I had almost forgotten the smell, the feel of it all,
The coming back home, with girls laughing like
    stars,
Their cheeks, holly berries, me kissing one,
Silent-tongued, soberly, by the long church wall;
Then back to the kitchen table, supper on the white
    cloth,
Cheese, bread, the home-made wine:
Symbols of the Night's joy, a holy feast.
And I wonder now, years gone, mother gone,
The boys and girls scattered, drifted away with the
    snowflakes,
Lamplight done, firelight over,
If the sounds of our singing in the streets are still
    there,
Those old times, still praising:
And now, a life-time of Decembers away from it
    all,
A branch of remembering holly spears my cheeks,
And I think it may be so;
Yes, I believe it may be so.

Leonard Clark

The children's carol

Here we come again, again, and here we come
   again,
Christmas is a single pearl swinging on a chain,
Christmas is a single flower in a barren wood,
Christmas is a single sail on the salty flood,
Christmas is a single star in the empty sky,
Christmas is a single song sung for charity.
Here we come again, again, to sing to you again,
Give a single penny that we may not sing in vain.

Eleanor Farjeon

The Coventry carol

Lully, lulla, you little tiny child,
Bye bye, lully lullay.
O sisters too,
How may we do
   For to preserve this day
This poor youngling,
For whom we do sing,
   Bye bye, lully lullay?

Herod, the king,
In his raging,
   Charged he had this day
His men of might,
In his own sight,
   All young children to slay.

That woe is me,
Poor child for thee!
   And ever morn and day,
For your parting
Neither say nor sing
   Bye bye, lully lullay!

December music

As I went into the city, clattering chimes
Carolled December music over the traffic
And I remembered my childhood, the times
Of deep snow, the same songs.

Cars meshed in the rain, horns snarled, brakes
Cursed against trolleys, and the neon evening
Blurred past my cold spectacles, the flakes
Of the iron songs scattered.

I stood near a corner drugstore trying to hear,
While all the weather broke to pouring water,
The drowned phrases between those coming clear
Though of course I knew all.

The notes my mind sang over would not do
To knit the shattered song as I wanted it,
Wanted it bell to bell as it once rang through
To its triumphant end.

It was no matter what I had left to believe
On a flooded pavement under a battering sign,
Clutching my hat while rain ran in my sleeve
And my bi-focals fogged.

It was only to think of my childhood, the deep
  snow,
The same songs, and Christmas Eve in the air,
And at home everyone in the world I knew
All together there.

Winfield Townley Scott

The wicked singers

And have you been out carol singing,
Collecting for the Old Folk's Dinner?

Oh yes indeed, oh yes indeed.

And did you sing all the Christmas numbers,
Every one a winner?

Oh yes indeed, oh yes indeed.

Good King Wenceslas, and Hark
The Herald Angels Sing?

Oh yes indeed, oh yes indeed.

And did you sing them loud and clear
And make the night sky ring?

Oh yes indeed, oh yes indeed.

And did you count up all the money?
Was it quite a lot?

Oh yes indeed, oh yes indeed.

And did you give it all to the Vicar,
Everything you'd got?

Certainly not, certainly not.

                                    Kit Wright

The rabbit's Christmas carol

I'm sick as a parrot,
I've lost me carrot,
I couldn't care less if it's
Christmas Day.

I'm sick as a parrot,
I've lost me carrot,
So get us a lettuce
Or . . . go away!

Kit Wright

The Christmas mouse

A Christmas mouse
Came to our house,
Looking for crumbs
That clumsy thumbs
Had dropped on the floor.
Under the door
He quietly crept
And bits not swept
He nibbled and sniffed,
'A Christmas gift,'
Old Mousie thought
And went and brought
His relations and friends
To share the ends
Of our Christmas feast.

Daphne Lister

Christmas

The bells of waiting Advent ring,
   The Tortoise stove is lit again
And lamp-oil light across the night
   Has caught the streaks of winter rain
In many a stained-glass window sheen
From Crimson Lake to Hooker's Green.

The holly in the windy hedge
   And round the Manor House the yew
Will soon be stripped to deck the ledge,
   The altar, font and arch and pew,
So that the villagers can say
'The church looks nice' on Christmas Day.

Provincial public houses blaze
   And Corporation tramcars clang,
On lighted tenements I gaze
   Where paper decorations hang,
And bunting in the red Town Hall
Says 'Merry Christmas to you all.'

And London shops on Christmas Eve
   Are strung with silver bells and flowers
As hurrying clerks the City leave
   To pigeon-haunted classic towers,
And marbled clouds go scudding by
The many-steepled London sky.

And girls in slacks remember Dad,
   And oafish louts remember Mum,
And sleepless children's hearts are glad,
   And Christmas-morning bells say 'Come!'
Even to shining ones who dwell
Safe in the Dorchester Hotel.

And is it true? And is it true,
   This most tremendous tale of all,
Seen in a stained-glass window's hue,
   A Baby in an ox's stall?
The Maker of the stars and sea
Become a Child on earth for me?

And is it true? For if it is,
   No loving fingers tying strings
Around those tissued fripperies,
   The sweet and silly Christmas things,
Bath salts and inexpensive scent
And hideous tie so kindly meant,

No love that in a family dwells,
   No carolling in frosty air,
Nor all the steeple-shaking bells
   Can with this single Truth compare –
That God was Man in Palestine
And lives today in Bread and Wine.

John Betjeman

Merry are the bells

Merry are the bells, and merry would they ring,
Merry was myself, and merry could I sing;
With a merry ding-dong, happy, gay, and free,
And a merry sing-song, happy let us be.

Little Christ Jesus

Now every Child that dwells on earth,
Stand up, stand up and sing:
The passing night has given birth
Unto the children's King.
Sing sweet as the flute,
Sing clear as the horn,
Sing joy of the Children,
Come Christmas the morn:
   *Little Christ Jesus
   Our brother is born.*

Now every star that dwells in sky,
Look down with shining eyes:
The night has dropped in passing by
A Star from Paradise.
Sing sweet as the flute,
Sing clear as the horn,
Sing joy of the Stars,
Come Christmas the morn:
  Little Christ Jesus
  Our brother is born.

Now every Beast that crops in field,
Breathe sweetly and adore:
The night has brought the richest yield
That ever the harvest bore.
Sing sweet as the flute,
Sing clear as the horn,
Sing joy of the Creatures,
Come Christmas the morn:
  Little Christ Jesus
  Our brother is born.

Now every Bird that flies in air,
Sing, raven, lark and dove:
The night has brooded on her lair
And fledged the Bird of love.
Sing sweet as the flute,
Sing clear as the horn,
Sing joy of the Birds,
Come Christmas the morn:
  Little Christ Jesus
  Our brother is born.

Now all the Angels of the Lord,
Rise up on Christmas Even:
The passing night will hear the Word
That is the voice of Heaven.
Sing sweet as the flute,
Sing clear as the horn,
Sing joy of the Angels,
Come Christmas the Morn:
 Little Christ Jesus
 Our brother is born.

Eleanor Farjeon

Christmas Day is drawing near

Now Christmas Day is drawing near at hand,
Pray serve the Lord and be at his command.
Oh for our portion God he will provide
And give a blessing to our souls beside.

Can you remember that man he was made of clay?
All in this world we have not got long to stay.
This wicked world will never give content
With all the blessings which our Lord God sent.

Down in the garden where flowers grow by ranks
Down on your knees and return the Lord God
    thanks;
Down on your knees, and pray both night and day
And leave off sin and leave off pride, I say.

So proud and lofty do some people go,
They've dressed themselves like puppets in a show;
They'll paste, they'll paint and dress with the idol
    stuff
As though God had not made them fine enough.

Come, come, Lord God, pray take me for your
    own,
Come, Jesus Christ, receive me to your throne.
Come, Holy Ghost, and cede it for us all
And crown my soul with the higher Trinity.

The shepherds' carol

We stood on the hills, Lady,
Our day's work done,
Watching the frosted meadows
That winter had won.

The evening was calm, Lady,
The air so still,
Silence more lovely than music
Folded the hill.

There was a star, Lady,
Shone in the night,
Larger than Venus it was
And bright, so bright.

Oh, a voice from the sky, Lady,
It seemed to us then
Telling of God being born
In the world of men.

And so we have come, Lady,
Our day's work done,
Our love, our hopes, ourselves
We give to your son.

The Eve of Christmas

It was the evening before the night
That Jesus turned from dark to light.

Joseph was walking round and round,
And yet he moved not on the ground.

He looked into the heavens, and saw
The pole stood silent, star on star.

He looked into the forest: there
The leaves hung dead upon the air.

He looked into the sea, and found
It frozen, and the lively fishes bound.

And in the sky, the birds that sang
Not in feathered clouds did hang.

Said Joseph: 'What is this silence all?'
An angel spoke: 'It is no thrall,

But is a sign of great delight:
The Prince of Love is born this night.'

And Joseph said: 'Where may I find
This wonder?' – 'He is all mankind,

Look, he is both farthest, nearest,
Highest and lowest, of all men the dearest.'

Then Joseph moved, and found the stars
Moved with him, and the evergreen airs,

The birds went flying, and the main
Flowed with its fishes once again.

And everywhere they went, they cried:
'Love lives, when all had died!'

In Excelsis Gloria!

James Kirkup

The three drovers

Across the plains one Christmas night, three
    drovers riding blythe and gay,
Looked up and saw a starry light, more radiant than
    the Milky Way;
And on their hearts such wonder fell, they sang with
    joy 'Noël! Noël!'

The air was dry with summer heat, and smoke was
    on the yellow moon;
But from the heavens, faint and sweet, came
    floating down a wondrous tune;
And, as they heard, they sang full well, those
    drovers three 'Noël! Noël!'

The black swans flew across the sky, the wild dog
    called across the plain,
The starry lustre blazed on high, still echoed on the
    heavenly strain;
And still they sang 'Noël! Noël!' those drovers three
    'Noël! Noël!'

John Wheeler

On Christmas Eve

On Christmas Eve I turned the spit,
I burnt my fingers, I feel it yet;
The little cock sparrow flew over the table,
The pot began to play with the ladle.

My Christmas list

A police car
A helicopter
A gun that goes pop
A Frisbee
A ball
An Action Man that won't stop
A torch
A guitar
A printing set with ink
A bouncer
A new bear
A submarine that won't sink
A sword
A typewriter
A stove so I can cook
A radio
A Wendy house
Another dinosaur book –
Of course, Father Christmas, it's clearly understood
That I'll only get *all* of this if I'm *specially* good.

Gyles Brandreth

The computer's first Christmas card

jollymerry
hollyberry
jollyberry
merryholly
happyjolly
jollyjelly
jellybelly
bellymerry
hollyheppy
jollyMolly
marryJerry
merryHarry
hoppyBarry
heppyJarry
boppyheppy
berryjorry
jorryjolly
moppyjelly

Mollymerry
Jerryjolly
bellyboppy
jorryhoppy
hollymoppy
Barrymerry
Jarryhappy
happyboppy
boppyjolly
jollymerry
merrymerry
merrymerry
merryChris
ammerryasa
Chrismerry
asMERRYCHR
YSANTHEMUM

Edwin Morgan

As Christmas draws nigh

Soon this little house I'll leave behind,
Yet I shall always find
It will ever be in my mind;
And as Christmas draws nigh
Always in my mind's eye,
The tree's so many pretty lights,
Its glittering tinsel so dazzling at night.
Outside, little snowflakes falling;
Upstairs, two little voices calling;
Little parcels beribboned and gay,
Under the tree ready for Christmas Day.
I step outside once more,
My lit-up window to adore.
A band is playing, lantern swaying,
'Auld Lang Syne' it seemed to be saying,
Remembering times not so very long ago,
And a dear mother once more.
I silently climb the stairs to bed
Where everyone's dreams are shed.

Elizabeth Humphreys

The oxen

Christmas Eve, and twelve of the clock.
   'Now they are all on their knees,'
An elder said as we sat in a flock
   By the embers in hearthside ease.

We pictured the meek mild creatures where
   They dwelt in their strawy pen,
Nor did it occur to one of us there
   To doubt they were kneeling then.

So fair a fancy few would weave
   In these years! Yet, I feel,
If someone said on Christmas Eve,
   'Come; see the oxen kneel

In the lonely barton by yonder coomb
   Our childhood used to know,'
I should go with him in the gloom,
   Hoping it might be so.

Thomas Hardy

The night before Christmas

'Twas the night before Christmas, when all through
   the house
Not a creature was stirring, not even a mouse;
The stockings were hung by the chimney with care,
In hopes that St Nicholas soon would be there;
The children were nestled all snug in their beds,
While visions of sugarplums danced in their heads;

And Mamma in her 'kerchief, and I in my cap,
Had just settled our brains for a long winter's nap;
When out on the lawn there arose such a clatter,
I sprang from the bed to see what was the matter.
Away to the window I flew like a flash,
Tore open the shutters and threw up the sash.

The moon, on the breast of the new-fallen snow,
Gave the lustre of midday to objects below,
When what to my wondering eyes should appear,
But a miniature sleigh, and eight tiny reindeer,
With a little old driver, so lively and quick,
I knew in a moment it must be St Nick.

More rapid than eagles his courses they came,
And he whistled and shouted, and called them by
   name;
'Now, Dasher! Now, Dancer! Now, Prancer and
   Vixen!
On, Comet! On, Cupid! On, Donner and Blitzen!
To the top of the porch! To the top of the wall!
Now, dash away! Dash away! Dash away all!'

As dry leaves that before the wild hurricane fly,
When they meet with an obstacle, mount to the sky;
So up to the housetop the coursers they flew,
With the sleigh full of toys, and St Nicholas, too.

And then, in a twinkling, I heard on the roof
The prancing and pawing of each little hoof –
As I drew in my head, and was turning around,
Down the chimney St Nicholas came with a bound.

He was dressed all in fur, from his head to his foot,
And his clothes were all tarnished with ashes and
    soot;
A bundle of toys he had flung on his back,
And he looked like a pedlar just opening his pack.
His eyes – how they twinkled! His dimples, how
    merry!
His cheeks were like roses, his nose like a cherry!

His droll little mouth was drawn up like a bow,
And the beard of his chin was as white as the snow;
The stump of a pipe he held tight in his teeth,
And the smoke it encircled his head like a wreath;
He had a broad face and a little round belly
That shook, when he laughed, like a bowl full of
    jelly.

He was chubby and plump, a right jolly old elf,
And I laughed, when I saw him, in spite of myself;
A wink of his eye and a twist of his head,
Soon gave me to know I had nothing to dread;
He spoke not a word, but went straight to his work,
And filled all the stockings; then turned with a jerk,

And laying his finger aside of his nose,
And giving a nod, up the chimney he rose;
He sprang to his sleigh, to his team gave a whistle,
And away they all flew like the down of a thistle.
But I heard him exclaim, ere he drove out of sight,
'Happy Christmas to all, and to all a good night!'

Clement C. Moore

Where's Rudolph?

As he pulled on his boots Santa spotted the note
That Rudolph had left on the table:

'If you want to find out where I'm having fun
Solve these 10 simple clues if you're able.
Every word starts with C,
This is followed by O.
The third letter spells the location
Where sleigh bells are tinkling
And my hooves are twinkling
Creating a yuletide sensation

For a message in secret use clue number one,
The second is forceful persuasion.
To live side by side without strife is the third
And the fourth is a regal occasion.
The fifth is a Russian,
Number six goes with chips
And clue seven is something to spend.
On the stage eight is worn,
Number nine crows at dawn
And with 10 we work for the same end.'

Answer: Please turn to page 98.

Kriss Kringle★

Just as the moon was fading
    Amid her misty rings,
And every stocking was stuffed
    With childhood's precious things,

Old Kriss Kringle looked round,
    And saw on the elm-tree bough,
High-hung an oriole's nest,
    Silent and empty now.

'Quite like a stocking,' he laughed,
    'Pinned up there on the tree!
Little I thought the birds
    Expected a present from me!'

Then Old Kriss Kringle, who loves
    A joke as well as the best,
Dropped a handful of flakes
    In the oriole's empty nest.

                        Thomas Bailey Aldrich

★[Kriss Kringle means Christ Child]

The solution to Rudolph's coded message on page 95:

1st clue	C O D E
2nd clue	C O E R C E
3rd clue	C O E X I S T
4th clue	C O R O N A T I O N
5th clue	C O S S A C K
6th clue	C O D
7th clue	C O I N
8th clue	C O S T U M E
9th clue	C O C K
10th clue	C O O P E R A T E

Rudolph, as you can see, was having a great time at the DEERS' DISCO!

At nine of the night I opened my door

At nine of the night I opened my door
That stands midway between moor and moor,
And all around me, silver-bright,
I saw that the world had turned to white.

Thick was the snow on field and hedge
And vanished was the river-sedge,
Where winter skilfully had wound
A shining scarf without a sound.

And as I stood and gazed my fill
A stable-boy came down the hill.
With every step I saw him take
Flew at his heel a puff of flake.

His brow was whiter than the hoar,
A beard of freshest snow he wore,
And round about him, snowflake starred,
A red horse-blanket from the yard.

In a red cloak I saw him go,
His back was bent, his step was slow,
And as he laboured through the cold
He seemed a hundred winters old.

I stood and watched the snowy head,
The whiskers white, the cloak of red.
'A Merry Christmas!' I heard him cry.
'The same to you, old friend,' said I.

Charles Causley

King John's Christmas

King John was not a good man –
    He had his little ways.
And sometimes no one spoke to him
    For days and days and days.
And men who came across him,
    When walking in the town,
Gave him a supercilious stare,
Or passed with noses in the air –
And bad King John stood dumbly there,
    Blushing beneath his crown.

King John was not a good man,
    And no good friends had he.
He stayed in every afternoon . . .
    But no one came to tea.
And, round about December,
    The cards upon his shelf
Which wished him lots of Christmas cheer,
And fortune in the coming year,
Were never from his near and dear,
    But only from himself.

King John was not a good man,
    Yet had his hopes and fears.
They'd given him no present now
    For years and years and years.
But every year at Christmas,
    While minstrels stood about,
Collecting tribute from the young
For all the songs they might have sung,
He stole away upstairs and hung
    A hopeful stocking out.

King John was not a good man,
    He lived his life aloof;
Alone he thought a message out
    While climbing up the roof.
He wrote it down and propped it
    Against the chimney stack:
'TO ALL AND SUNDRY – NEAR AND FAR –
F. CHRISTMAS IN PARTICULAR.'
And signed it not 'Johannes R.'
    But very humbly, 'JACK.'

'I want some crackers,
    And I want some candy;
I think a box of chocolates
    Would come in handy;
I don't mind oranges,
    I do like nuts!
And I SHOULD like a pocket-knife
    That really cuts.
And, oh! Father Christmas, if you love me at all,
Bring me a big, red india-rubber ball!'

King John was not a good man –
    He wrote this message out,
And got him to his room again,
    Descending by the spout.
And all that night he lay there,
    A prey to hopes and fears.
'I think that's him a-coming now,'
    (Anxiety bedewed his brow.)
'He'll bring one present, anyhow –
    The first I've had for years.'

'Forget about the crackers,
    And forget about the candy;
I'm sure a box of chocolates
    Would never come in handy;
I don't like oranges,
    I don't want nuts,
And I HAVE got a pocket-knife
That almost cuts.
But, oh! Father Christmas, if you love me at all,
Bring me a big, red india-rubber ball!'

King John was not a good man –
    Next morning when the sun
Rose up to tell a waiting world
    That Christmas had begun,
And people seized their stockings,
    And opened them with glee,
And crackers, toys and games appeared,
And lips with sticky sweets were smeared,
King John said grimly: 'As I feared,
    Nothing again for me!'

'I did want crackers,
    And I did want candy;
I know a box of chocolates
    Would come in handy;
I do love oranges,
    I did want nuts.
I haven't got a pocket-knife –
    Not one that cuts.
And, oh! if Father Christmas had loved me at all,
He would have brought a big, red india-rubber
    ball!'

King John stood by the window,
　　And frowned to see below
The happy bands of boys and girls
　　All playing in the snow.
A while he stood there watching,
　　And envying them all . . .
When through the window big and red
There hurtled by his royal head,
And bounced and fell upon the bed,
　　An india-rubber ball!

AND OH, FATHER CHRISTMAS
　　MY BLESSINGS ON YOU FALL
　　　FOR BRINGING HIM
　　　A BIG, RED,
　　　INDIA-RUBBER
　　　BALL!

A. A. Milne

Has Father Christmas forgotten me?

It was Christmas Eve.
I knew Father Christmas
was mum and dad.
I knew he didn't come down the chimney
and instead
they came through the door.
I knew it didn't all come out of a sack
but instead
they left a heap of stuff at the end of the bed.
I knew it, I knew it, I knew it.
What I didn't know was what was going to be
    in the heap.
But I went to sleep
so then I woke up.
Nothing.
So I went to sleep
so then I woke up.
Nothing –
was that piece of paper there before?
Must have been.
So I went to sleep
so then I woke up.
Nothing – except for that bit of paper.
So I went to sleep
so then I woke up.
Nothing –
and it's morning.
Has Father Christmas
    forgotten me?
I mean, mum and dad.

Get up.
Feeling bad.
Feeling worse than bad.
Terrible.
Nearly crying.
The piece of paper –
what is it?
It's a picture of a bike
and underneath it, it says:
DOWNSTAIRS.
So it's rush–rush downstairs,
front room,
and there it was,
propped up against a chair
in front of the telly.
Big and shining.
Of course,
Father Christmas couldn't stuff a bike
down the chimney, could he?

Michael Rosen

Santa go home

My fellow parents,
The time has come
To realize that we've been dumb,
That century in
And century out
We have been hooked like silly trout,
That as our bank accounts have dwindled,
We have been hoodwinked,
Gypped, and swindled –
The victims of a confidence game
So blatant
We should blush with shame.
Who,
Though his banker eyes him dourly,
Doth crack his nest egg
Prematurely?
Who with the hungry loan shark battles
And pledges all his goods and chattels?
Who cons,
Until his vision fogs,
The endless Christmas catalogues?
Who crawls, exhausted,
On all fours
Through toy-shops
And department stores?
Who burns the lonely midnight taper
In futile struggle
With wrapping paper,
Entangled fast
From toe to head

In writhing ribbons green and red?
Who toils
From Christmas Eve to Morn
The tree to lavishly adorn?
Who's taken months of loving care
To stuff those stockings hanging there?
Who, bedded at five,
At six doth rise,
Waked by impatient childish cries?
Who can this selfless mortal be?
I'll tell you who:
It's you and me.
Who gets the gratitude and applause?
I'll tell you who:
    It's
       SANTA
          CLAUS

Ogden Nash

Christmas is really for the children

Christmas is really
for the children.
Especially for children
who like animals, stables,
stars and babies wrapped
in swaddling clothes.
Then there are wise men,
kings in fine robes,
humble shepherds and a
hint of rich perfume.

Easter is not really
for the children
unless accompanied by a
cream-filled egg.
It has whips, blood, nails,
a spear and allegations
of body-snatching.
It involves politics, God
and the sins of the world.
It is not good for people
of a nervous disposition.
They would do better to
think on rabbits, chickens
and the first snowdrop
of spring.
Or they'd do better to
wait for a re-run of

Christmas without asking
too many questions about
what Jesus did when he grew up
or whether there's any connection.

Steve Turner

A childhood Christmas

*(When my daughters were aged two
and three years old they inspired this poem.)*

I remember so
Ten years ago,
That Christmas morn,
Before the dawn,
My little girls
(My tiny 'pearls'),
Awoke with glee
And crept to see,
If 'he' had been
And not been mean.
We heard their cries,
Their gasps and sighs.
We heard their feet a–patter,
Along with childish chatter.
Then silence. No tussle,
Not even paper rustle
Impatient to see more,
I tip–toed to the door.
Two gold–haired babes
('Midst gifts arrayed

In piles upon the floor)
Stood; as in awe,
No gifts undone,
Their delight was won
By pretty paper shapes
And glittery Christmas tapes.
They couldn't comprehend;
So my hand I had to lend
To show them more
Inside those shapes upon the floor.

Andrea May

My father played the melodeon

(from *A Christmas Childhood*)

My father played the melodeon
Outside at our gate;
There were stars in the morning east
And they danced to his music.

Across the wild bogs his melodeon called
To Lennons and Callans.
As I pulled on my trousers in a hurry
I knew some strange thing had happened.

Outside in the cow-house my mother
Made the music of milking;
The light of her stable-lamp was a star
And the frost of Bethlehem made it twinkle.

A water-hen screeched in the bog,
Mass-going feet
Crunched the wafer-ice on the pot-holes,
Somebody wistfully twisted the bellows wheel.

My child poet picked out the letters
On the grey stone,
In silver the wonder of a Christmas townland,
The winking glitter of a frosty dawn.

Cassiopeia was over
Cassidy's hanging hill,
I looked and three whin bushes rode across
The horizon – the Three Wise Kings.

An old man passing said:
'Can't he make it talk' –
The melodeon. I hid in the doorway
And tightened the belt of my box-pleated coat.

I nicked six nicks on the door-post
With my penknife's big blade –
There was a little one for cutting tobacco.
And I was six Christmasses of age.

My father played the melodeon,
My mother milked the cows,
And I had a prayer like a white rose pinned
On the Virgin Mary's blouse.

Patrick Kavanagh

Sweets for Christmas morn

Apples for the little ones
And sweets for Christmas morn,
A dear blue bonnet for my wife
And I love barley corn.

Clyde Watson

Christmas Day

Small girls on trikes
Bigger on bikes
Collars on tykes

Looking like cads
Patterned in plaids
Scarf–wearing dads

Chewing a choc
Mum in a frock
Watches the clock

Knocking in pans
Fetching of grans
Gathering of clans

Hissing from tins
Sherries and gins
Upping of chins

Corks making pops
'Just a few drops'
Watering of chops

All this odd joy
Tears at a broken toy
Just for the birth long ago of a boy

Roy Fuller

A Christmas blessing

God bless the master of this house,
   The mistress also,
And all the little children
   That round the table go;
And all your kin and kinsfolk,
   That dwell both far and near:
I wish you a Merry Christmas
   And a Happy New Year.

We wish you a Merry Christmas

We wish you a Merry Christmas.
We wish you a Merry Christmas.
We wish you a Merry Christmas
And a Happy New Year.

Good tidings we bring
For you and your kin.
We wish you a Merry Christmas
And a Happy New Year.

Now bring us figgy pudding.
Now bring us figgy pudding.
Now bring us figgy pudding.
Now bring some right here!

We won't go until we get it.
We won't go until we get it.
We won't go until we get it.
So bring some right here!

We wish you a Merry Christmas.
We wish you a Merry Christmas.
We wish you a Merry Christmas.
And a Happy New Year.

Christmas bells

I heard the bells on Christmas day
Their old familiar carols play,
    And wild and sweet
    The words repeat,
Of 'Peace on earth, good will to men!'

And thought how, as the day had come,
The belfries of all Christendom
    Had rolled along
    The unbroken song,
Of 'Peace on earth, good will to men!'

Till ringing, singing on its way,
The world revolved from night to day –
    A voice, a chime,
    A chant sublime,
Of 'Peace on earth, good will to men!'

And in despair I bowed my head;
'There is no peace on earth,' I said,
    'For hate is strong
    And mocks the song
Of peace on earth, good will to men!'

Then pealed the bells more loud and deep:
'God is not dead; nor doth he sleep!
    The wrong shall fail,
    The right prevail,
With peace on earth, goodwill to men!'

Henry Wadsworth Longfellow

I saw three ships

I saw three ships come sailing by,
   On Christmas Day, on Christmas Day,
I saw three ships come sailing by,
   On Christmas Day in the morning.

And who was in those ships all three,
   On Christmas Day, on Christmas Day,
And who was in those ships all three,
   On Christmas Day in the morning?

Our Saviour Christ and His Lady,
   On Christmas Day, on Christmas Day,
Our Saviour Christ and His Lady,
   On Christmas Day in the morning.

Oh! they sailed into Bethlehem,
   On Christmas Day, on Christmas Day,
Oh! they sailed into Bethlehem,
   On Christmas Day in the morning.

And all the bells on earth shall ring,
   On Christmas Day, on Christmas Day,
And all the bells on earth shall ring,
   On Christmas Day in the morning.

And all the angels in Heaven shall sing,
  On Christmas Day, on Christmas Day,
And all the angels in Heaven shall sing,
  On Christmas Day in the morning.

And all the souls on earth shall sing,
  On Christmas Day, on Christmas Day,
And all the souls on earth shall sing,
  On Christmas Day in the morning.

Moonless darkness stands between

Moonless darkness stands between.
Past, O Past, no more be seen!
But the Bethlehem star may lead me
To the sight of Him who freed me
From the self that I have been.
Make me pure, Lord: Thou art holy;
Make me meek, Lord: Thou wert lowly;
Now beginning, and alway:
Now begin, on Christmas Day.

Gerard Manley Hopkins

Love came down at Christmas

Love came down at Christmas,
  Love all lovely, love divine,
Love was born at Christmas,
  Star and angels gave the sign.

Worship we the Godhead,
  Love incarnate, love divine;
Worship we our Jesus:
  But wherewith for sacred sign?

Love shall be our token,
  Love be yours and love be mine,
Love to God and all men,
  Love for plea and gift and sign.

Christina Rossetti

Christmastime

The fire, with well-dried logs supplied,
Went roaring up the chimney wide;
The huge hall-table's oaken face,
Scrubbed till it shone the day to grace,
Bore then upon its massive board
No mark to part the squire and lord.
Then was brought in the lusty brawn,
By old blue-coated serving-man;
Then the grim boar's head frowned on high,
Crested with bays and rosemary.
Well can the green-garbed ranger tell,
How, when, and where, the monster fell:
What dogs before his death he tore,
And all the baiting of the boar.
The wassail round in good brown bowls,
Garnished with ribbons, blithely trowls.
There the huge sirloin reeked; hard by
Plum-porridge stood, and Christmas pie
Nor failed old Scotland to produce,
At such high-tide, her savoury goose.

Sir Walter Scott

Christmas pie

Lo! now is come our joyfullest feast!
   Let every man be jolly;
Each room with ivy leaves is dressed,
   And every post with holly.

Now all our neighbours' chimneys smoke,
   And Christmas blocks are burning;
Their ovens they with bakemeats choke,
   And all their spits are turning.

Without the door let sorrow lie,
   And if for cold it hap to die,
We'll bury it in a Christmas pie,
   And ever more be merry.

George Wither

Yule! Yule!

Yule! Yule!
Three puddings in a pool;
Crack nuts and cry Yule!

The wassail bowl

The brown bowl,
The merry brown bowl,
As it goes round-about,
   Fill,
   Still,
Let the world say what it will,
And drink your fill all out.

The deep can,
The merry deep can,
As you do freely quaff
   Sing,
   Fling,
Be merry as a king,
And sound a lusty laugh.

Snapdragon

Here he comes with flaming bowl,
Don't he mean to take his toll,
   Snip! Snap! Dragon.
Take care you don't take too much,
Be not greedy in your clutch,
   Snip! Snap! Dragon.

With his blue and lapping tongue
Many of you will be stung,
   Snip! Snap! Dragon.
For he snaps at all that comes
Snatching at his feast of plums,
   Snip! Snap! Dragon.

But old Christmas makes him come,
Though he looks so fee! fo! fum!
   Snip! Snap! Dragon.
Don't ever fear him, but be bold,
Out he goes, his flames are cold,
   Snip! Snap! Dragon.

St George and the Dragon

(A traditional Cornish Christmas play)

Characters

SAINT GEORGE   KING OF EGYPT

THE DRAGON   TURKISH KNIGHT

FATHER CHRISTMAS   THE GIANT TURPIN

THE DOCTOR

Enter the TURKISH KNIGHT:

Open your doors, and let me in,
I hope your favours I shall win;
Whether I rise or whether I fall,
I'll do my best to please you all.
St George is here, and swears he will come in,
And if he does, I know he'll pierce my skin.
If you will not believe what I do say,
Let Father Christmas come in – clear the way.

[*Retires*]

Enter FATHER CHRISTMAS:

Here come I, old Father Christmas,
　　Welcome, or welcome not,
I hope old Father Christmas
　　Will never be forgot.

I am not come here to laugh or to jeer,
But for a pocketfull of money, and a skinful of beer,
If you will not believe what I do say,
Come in, the King of Egypt! – clear the way!

Enter the KING OF EGYPT:

Here I, the King of Egypt, boldly do appear,
St George, St George, walk in, my only son and
　　heir.
Walk in, my son St George, and boldly act thy part,
That all the people here may see thy wond'rous art.

Enter SAINT GEORGE:

Here come I, St George, from Britain did I spring,
I'll fight the Dragon bold, my wonders to begin.
I'll clip his wings, he shall not fly;
I'll cut him down, or else I die.

Enter THE DRAGON:

Who's he that seeks the Dragon's blood,
And calls so angry, and so loud?
That English dog, will he before me stand?
I'll cut him down with my courageous hand.
With my long teeth, and scurvy jaw,
Of such I'd break up half a score,
And stay my stomach, till I'd more.

SAINT GEORGE *and* THE DRAGON *fight; the latter is killed.*

FATHER CHRISTMAS:

Is there a doctor to be found
All ready, near at hand,
To cure a deep and deadly wound,
And make the champion stand?

Enter DOCTOR:

Oh! yes, there is a doctor to be found
    All ready, near at hand,
To cure a deep and deadly wound,
    And make the champion stand.

FATHER CHRISTMAS:

What can you cure?

DOCTOR:

All sorts of diseases,
Whatever you pleases,
The phthisic, the palsy, and the gout;
If the devil's in, I'll blow him out.

FATHER CHRISTMAS:
What is your fee?

DOCTOR:
Fifteen pound, it is my fee,
The money to lay down.
But, as 'tis such a rogue as thee,
I cure for ten pound.

I carry a little bottle of alicumpane;
    Here Jack, take a little of my flip flop,
    Pour it down thy tip top;
Rise up and fight again.

THE DOCTOR *performs his cure, the fight is renewed, and*
THE DRAGON *again killed*.

SAINT GEORGE:
Here am I, St George,
    That worthy champion bold,
And with my sword and spear
    I won three crowns of gold.
I fought the fiery dragon,
    And brought him to the slaughter;
By that I won fair Sabra,
    The King of Egypt's daughter.
Where is the man, that now will me defy?
I'll cut his giblets full of holes, and make his buttons
    fly.

The TURKISH KNIGHT *advances*:
Here come I, the Turkish Knight,
Come from the Turkish land to fight.
I'll fight St George, who is my foe,
I'll make him yield before I go;
He brags to such a high degree,
He thinks there's none can do the like of he.

SAINT GEORGE:
Where is the Turk, that will before me stand?
I'll cut him down with my courageous hand.

They fight, the KNIGHT *is overcome, and falls on one
knee.*

TURKISH KNIGHT:
Oh! pardon me, St George, pardon of thee I crave,
Oh! pardon me this night, and I will be thy slave.

SAINT GEORGE:
No pardon shalt thou have, while I have foot to
stand,
So rise thee up again, and fight out sword in hand.

They fight again, and the KNIGHT *is killed.* FATHER
CHRISTMAS *calls for* THE DOCTOR, *with whom the
same dialogue occurs as before, and the cure is performed.*

Enter THE GIANT TURPIN:
Here come I, the Giant, bold Turpin is my name,
And all the nations round do tremble at my fame.
Where'er I go, they tremble at my sight,
No lord or champion long with me would fight.

SAINT GEORGE:

Here's one that dares to look thee in the face,
And soon will sent thee to another place.

They fight, and THE GIANT *is killed; medical aid is called
in as before, and the cure performed by* THE DOCTOR, *to
whom then is given a basin of girdy grout and a kick,
and driven out.*

FATHER CHRISTMAS:

Now, ladies and gentlemen, your sport is most
   ended,
So prepare for the hat, which is highly commended.
The hat it would speak, if it had but a tongue;
Come throw in your money, and think it no wrong.

[*Play ends*]

For them

Before you bid, for Christmas' sake,
   Your guests to sit at meat,
Oh please to save a little cake
   For them that have no treat.

Before you go down party-dressed
   In silver gown or gold,
Oh please to send a little vest
   To them that still go cold.

Before you give your girl and boy
   Gay gifts to be undone,
Oh please to spare a little toy
   To them that will have none.

Before you gather round the tree
   To dance the day about,
Oh please to give a little glee
   To them that go without.

Eleanor Farjeon

At Christmas be merry

At Christmas be merry, and thankful withal,
And feast your poor neighbours, the great with the
   small.

Thomas Tusser

Keeping Christmas

How will you your Christmas keep?
Feasting, fasting, or asleep?
Will you laugh or will you pray,
Or will you forget the day?

Be it kept with joy or prayer,
Keep of either some to spare;
Whatsoever brings the day,
Do not keep but give away.

Eleanor Farjeon

No pretty Christmas toys

Think upon the girls and boys
Who get no pretty Christmas toys,
Who suffer want, and cold, and care,
And help them, both by alms and prayer.

From a Victorian Christmas card

A stormy night one Christmas day

It was a stormy night
one Christmas day
as they fell awake
on the Santa Fe

Turkey, jelly
and the ship's old cook
all jumped out
of a recipe book

The jelly wobbled
the turkey gobbled
and after them both
the old cook hobbled

Gobbler gobbled
Hobbler's Wobbler.
Hobbler gobbled
Wobbler's Gobbler.

Gobbly-gobbler
gobbled Wobbly
Hobbly-hobbler
Gobbled Gobbly.

Gobble gobbled
Hobble's Wobble
Hobble gobbled
gobbled Wobble.

gobble gobble
wobble wobble
hobble gobble
wobble gobble

Michael Rosen

Christmas Thank You's

Dear Auntie
Oh, what a nice jumper
I've always adored powder blue
and fancy you thinking of
orange and pink
for the stripes
how clever of you!

Dear Uncle
The soap is
terrific
So
useful
and such a kind thought and
how did you guess that
I'd just used the last of
the soap that last Christmas brought

Dear Gran
Many thanks for the hankies
Now I really can't wait for the flu
and the daisies embroidered
in red round the 'M'
for Michael
how
thoughtful of you!

Dear Cousin
What socks!
and the same sort you wear
so you must be
the last word in style
and I'm certain you're right that the
luminous green
will make me stand out a mile

Dear Sister
I quite understand your concern
it's a risk sending jam in the post
But I think I've pulled out
all the big bits
of glass
so it won't taste too sharp
spread on toast

Dear Grandad
Don't fret
I'm delighted
So *don't* think your gift will
offend
I'm not at all hurt
that you gave up this year
and just sent me
a fiver
to spend

Mick Gowar

Epiphany

Down with the rosemary, and so
Down with the bays and mistletoe;
Down with the holly, ivy, all
Wherewith you dressed the Christmas hall;
That so the superstitious find
No one least branch there left behind;
For look, how many leaves there be
Neglected, there – maids, trust to me –
So many goblins you shall see.

Kindle the Christmas brand, and then
Till sunset let it burn;
Which quenched, then lay it up again
Till Christmas next return.
Parts must be kept wherewith to tend
The Christmas log next year,
And where it's saftely kept, the fiend
Can do no mischief there.

End now the white loaf and the pie,
And let all sport with Christmas die.

Robert Herrick

After Christmas

There were lots on the farm,
But the turkeys are gone.
They were gobbling alarm:
There were lots on the farm,
Did they come to some harm,
Like that poor little fawn?
There were lots on the farm,
But the turkeys are gone.

David McCord

Twelfth Night carol

Here we come a–whistling through the fields so
        green;
Here we come a–singing, so fair to be seen.
    God send you happy, God send you happy,
    Pray God send you a happy New Year!

Bring out your little table and spread it with a cloth,
Bring out your jug of milk, likewise your
        Christmas loaf.
    God send you happy, God send you happy,
    Pray God send you a happy New Year!

God bless the master of this house, God bless the
        mistress too;
And all the little children that round the table go.
    God send you happy, God send you happy,
    Pray God send you a happy New Year!

To bed now . . .

Soft falls the snow,
The coals burn low,
Little Jacob's asleep on my knee;
My story ends here
For midnight is near:
To bed now, one-two-three!

Clyde Watson

Acknowledgements

The compilers and publisher wish to thank the following for permission to use copyright material in this anthology.

The publishers have made every effort to trace copyright holders. If we have inadvertently omitted to acknowledge anyone we should be grateful if this could be brought to our attention for correction at the first opportunity.

Bell and Hyman for 'Mincemeat' by Elizabeth Gould, from *The Book of a Thousand Poems*.

Gyles Brandreth for 'My Christmas List'.

Jonathan Cape Limited and the Executors of the Estate of C. Day Lewis for 'The Christmas Tree' by C. Day Lewis from *Collected Poems 1954* (Hogarth Press).

Carcanet Press Limited for 'The Computer's First Christmas Card' by Edwin Morgan, from *Poems of Thirty Years*, and for 'Blue Toboggans' by Edwin Morgan from *From Glasgow to Saturn*.

Chappell Music for 'The Three Drovers' by John Wheeler, from *Five Australian Christmas Carols*.

Collins Publishers for 'Christmas Thank You's' by Mick Gowar, from *Swings and Roundabouts*.

Curtis Brown for 'Santa Go Home' copyright © 1966, 1967 by Ogden Nash and 'Winter Morning' copyright © Ogden Nash.

J. M. Dent and Sons Limited for 'When All the World is Full of Snow' by N. M. Bodecker, from *Hurry, Hurry, Mary Dear*.

André Deutsch for 'A Stormy Night One Christmas Day' by Michael Rosen, from *Mind Your Own Business*.

Dobson Books Limited for 'Singing in the Streets' by Leonard Clark from *Singing in the Streets*.

Fontana Paperbacks for 'The Wicked Singers' from *Rabbiting On* by Kit Wright.

Granada Publishing Limited for 'little silent Christmas tree' by e. e. cummings from *Complete Poems 1913–1962*.

Harrap Limited for 'After Christmas' by David McCord from *Mr Bider's Spidery Garden*.

David Higham Associates Limited for 'Advice to a Child', 'For Them', 'The Children's Carol', 'Little Christ Jesus', and 'Keeping Christmas', by Eleanor Farjeon, and for 'Something Beautiful and New and Strange' and 'Winter Morning' by Clive Sansom.

The Hutchinson Publishing Group Limited for 'Planting Mistletoe' by Ruth Pitter from *End of Drought*.

Mrs Katherine B. Kavanagh for 'My Father Played the Melodeon' taken from the poem 'A Christmas Childhood' from *Collected Poems of Patrick Kavanagh*.

James Kirkup for 'The Eve of Christmas'.

The Literary Trustees of Walter de la Mare and the Society of Authors as their representative for 'Snowing' and 'Mistletoe' by Walter de la Mare.

Macmillan Publishers for 'Apples for the Little Ones' and 'To Bed Now' by Clyde Watson from *Father Fox's Penny Rhymes*.

Methuen Children's Books and McClelland and Stewart Limited for 'King John's Christmas' by A. A. Milne from *Now We Are Six*.

John Murray Publishers for 'Christmas' by John Betjeman, from *Collected Poems*.

Oxford University Press for 'Christmas Day' by Roy

A note from the Editors

You have probably noticed that in some books of verse there are many poems written by 'Anon' and 'Unknown'. But who are, or rather *were*, they? Well, they were poets who were so mysterious that today we do not know their names. They are simply *unknown* – or *anonymous*, which means the same thing. So where a name does not appear at the end of a poem in this book, you can be sure that the poet's identity is still a mystery.

Index of first lines